Until the Last Light Leaves

Pat
   Thanks for the support. Hope you go
for some of these.

         Best
         Tony Gloeggler
         10/20/15

Also by Tony Gloeggler

ONE ON ONE (Pearl Editions, 1999)

ONE WISH LEFT (Pavement Saw Press 2002, Second Edition, 2007)

MY OTHER LIFE (Jane Street Press, 2004)

GREATEST HITS (Pudding House Publications, 2009)

THE LAST LIE (NYQ Books, 2010)

TONY COME BACK AUGUST (Bittersweet Editions, 2015)

Until the Last Light Leaves

Tony Gloeggler

The New York Quarterly Foundation, Inc.
New York, New York

NYQ Books™ is an imprint of The New York Quarterly Foundation, Inc.

The New York Quarterly Foundation, Inc.
P. O. Box 2015
Old Chelsea Station
New York, NY 10113

www.nyq.org

First Edition

Set in New Baskerville

Layout and Design by Raymond P. Hammond
Cover photo by Darcy Flanagan

Library of Congress Control Number: 2015946407

ISBN: 978-1-63045-007-6

Until the Last Light Leaves

Acknowledgments

Thank you Raymond Hammond for giving these poems a gathering place and for doing all the work it took to put this collection together. Thank you Michael Flanagan and Ted Jonathan for your patience and enthusiasm in reading the first, last and too many in-between versions of these poems. Thank you hot shot award winning high school photographer Darcy Flanagan for letting me use your photo for the cover while I can still afford your prices. Thank you Patricia Smith for your encouragement, support and mostly for meaning all the generous thoughts and words you fit into the blurb. Thank you William Packard for taking me and my poems in, making me a part of the *New York Quarterly* thirty or so years ago. And thanks to anyone who reads these poems.

Thanks to the editors of the following journals who published some of the poems in this collection:

Massachusetts Review, Skidrow Penthouse, The Ledge, The Bridge, The New York Quarterly, Lactuca, Turnstile, Quercus, Mudfish, Trailer Park Quarterly, Graffiti Rag, Barbaric Yawp, Rattle, Poet Lore, Washington Square, Little Eagle Re/Verse, The Gathering Of The Tribes, Black Bear Review, Kaleidoscope, Poetic Diversity, Paterson Literary Review, Ted Kooser's Newspaper Feed, Mas Tequila Review, Nerve Cowboy, Misfit, 2 Bridges Review, Newtown Literary, Trajectory, Exit 7, Juked, Washington Square, The Raleigh Review, Mangrove, Columbia Poetry Review, The Chiron Review.

.

This one's for the people who have come and gone, lived and worked at Warren Residence since its opening in November 1979.
Especially Larry.

But mostly, of course, it is for Joshua. With nothing but love. All of the time.

Contents

Until the Last Light Leaves

THE WAY A WORLD CAN CHANGE

Start with a letter from a woman
who disappeared, broke
your heart eight years ago.
Her life's a stolen car,
an escape from a cult,
a sperm bank son, six
years old, autistic.
She's not sure why
she's writing. Don't laugh,
it says, she's moving
to Maine, trying to find
herself and she remembers
the time spent with you
as happy, stable.

Read it again. Write back,
edit it like a new poem.
You're working the same
job, there are still no
pictures on your walls,
your first full length collection
will be published in January.
You like the name Jesse, ask
if he has her clear blue eyes.
Hope that when she finds herself
it will be the woman you loved.
Write. Call. Anytime.

Answer the phone. It's her,
Helen. Talk until Jesse
screams too loud and wrestles
the phone from her hands.
Fly Jet Blue. Kiss
in the garage like kids

at recess. Eat at a diner.
Hold hands, touch knees
under the table. Make love,
fuck on her futon until
it's time to pick Jesse up
from school. Try not
to feel so warm, so lucky.

Eleven months later, Brooklyn.
Helen, Jesse, you, living
in an apartment you can barely
afford. He's sick, she's left
for her new job and you're half
asleep. The phone rings.
Helen's scared. She says
to turn the TV on. You watch
the buildings burn and fall,
wish you could hold her
as you feel Jesse's head
for fever. She'll be home
soon as she can. Be careful.
She loves you. Quietly
lie down next to Jesse.

Two nights later, go outside.
The sidewalks are empty,
hushed. Something is still
burning. You hold Helen's
hand, watch Jesse graze
his fingers against fences.
Flags drape every third
porch. A cat rattles
a trash can, a dog growls
and your neck tenses

with each sound. You pull
Helen closer. Jesse darts
into Ocean Parkway. A car
swerves, skids to a stop.
The driver drops his head
to the steering wheel,
covers it with his arms.
She crouches, cries
into Jesse's shoulder.
You sit on the curb,
hug your knees.
End here, please.

DOWN'S SYNDROME

The nurse hands the newborn
to his mother. Her husband stands
by the window, pats his pockets
like a cop searching a suspect,
finds his cigarettes and leaves

the room. Mary keeps still,
afraid she might wake the baby.
She counts fingers, toes,
nods each time she reaches
ten. She examines his thick

neck, slack jaw, fat rutted tongue
and wants to touch, stroke
his head, press her thumbs
into the small soft spot, squeeze
until her son screams sirens.

DOWN'S SYNDROME II

Behind the glass wall
nine babies sleep
in tiny cribs. Wrinkled
with mostly bald heads
they all look the same.
He skims four index cards
before he finds the one
with his son's name
on it. The night nurse
walks over, touches
his arm. "Anything
I can do?" He shakes
his head no. She says,
"You may as well go
home, get some rest.
Your wife will sleep
through the night."
He nods, imagines
himself back home
lying on his side
of the bed, eyes
wide open. He hears
traffic on the street,
heat pipes cough,
the kitchen sink drip.
He gets up, slips
into moccasins, smokes
two cigarettes, paces
into the baby's room,
rocks the bassinet, strokes
the cotton comforter, nudges
the Mickey Mouse mobile
and watches it spin.

BALANCE

My first visit, we spent
hours playing catch. Moving
like a squirrel on a telephone
wire, Jesse stood at the top
of the stairs rolling down
fat colorful balls. Standing
at the bottom and under
handing them back, I kept
asking Helen, you sure
he won't fall. Leaning
forward and grasping
onto a rail with one hand
he caught my soft tosses,
then let the ball go,
bent his head at crazy
different angles, intently
watched the ball, its spins
and bounces, descend
until it landed safely
in my sure hands.

I'd wrap a few days
around a weekend, spend
half of it like a teenager
in love, the other half
as a husband, a father,
watching Jesse climb
monkey bars, tumble
roll down hills, waiting
in doctors' offices, sitting
through school meetings
and holding Helen's hand
as she requested, begged,
screamed for and eventually

cried every time they denied
Jesse the special speech
therapy he needed daily.

Helen was falling fiercely
in love with me again
and the fairy tale idea
of a steadier life,
a life that would push
her past further behind.
I was falling too, in steady
slow motion, floating,
sailing closer to her,
feeling happy, blessed
and no doubt in love,
but scared of her roller
coaster ways, losing
control of my time
and trying to figure out
how it could all fit.

After struggling to bathe
a slippery screaming Jesse,
she'd fall asleep quickly
with her head pressed
against my chest. I'd lie
awake, listen to her breath
go out and in. Would I move
to England immediately
if they discovered a cure
for autism tomorrow?
Could I find the perfect
Brooklyn school for Jesse?

Could we afford special
services? Would I find time
to write? Could she ever
love me nearly as much
as she loves Jesse?
Would that be enough?

CREEDMORE

The stale urine, Lysol smell
stings my nose, my eyes
every time I walk inside. I tie
back my hair in a pony tail, tuck it
under my blue denim collar,
walk in room 319. Lee kneels
on a green gym mat, rocks back
and forth, flaps his fingers
as high pitched shrieks squeeze
through clenched teeth. Dennis,
seventeen yesterday, bends over
the table and drips drool down
his chin, slicks back his tangled
black hair with foamy spit.
Jim picks scabs off his left wrist,
sticks them in his mouth, chews
slowly. Joey jumps up and down
in the corner, pumps his big cock
with two tight fists, mumbles "mutha
fucka, mutha mutha" and punches
the side of his head every fifteen
minutes. I turn on the radio,
Dylan drones through fits
of static, "How does it feel?"

TIME OUT

Lin, if you wouldn't bite the ball
every damn time I hand it to you,
you could play fullback on my nephew's
Pop Warner team. I could watch your crew cut
butt through goal line stands for six points.
Twelve year old cheerleaders would be doing splits
and you'd be getting and giving high fives.
After, you could hang out in the grandstand.

Instead, we sit in this time out room.
I unstrap your protective helmet,
spoon feed you three finely chopped tablets
hidden in lemon Jell-o, watch you swallow
every mouthful. And maybe you won't crack
your head against the bedroom wall again tonight.

THOUGHTS AND THEORIES OF SPACE AND DISTANCE WHEN YOUR GIRLFRIEND SAYS SHE WANTS TO LIVE TOGETHER AND YOU SAY YES, MAYBE IN THE SUMMER

You think there's some kind of formula
involving miles per hour and car lengths
one needs to keep between your Jeep
and the gray mini van full of kids
making faces out the tinted back window
that equals safety in case of sudden stops.
But you don't know. You don't drive and never
could figure out what X equaled in school.

Five days a week, you stand on a platform
with people who glance at watches, lean
over tracks and look into the dark tunnel,
hoping. You think they should be careful,
stay behind the yellow line. Last night, a man
jumped or fell in front of the train you were on.
You felt the lurch and watched mouths gasping
and screaming, hands dropping packages,
oranges rolling on the ground. Everyone
had to turn away. One woman crumpled
slow motion into a crouch, fell against
a pole. The cops and EMS workers arrived
quicker than seemed possible. Still, the news
led with a decapitated, unidentified man.

Today, when your train comes, you find
a prime standing spot and test your friend's
theory that every rush hour subway car
carries at least one woman you could love
for a long time. No, it's not the blonde
stunning everyone as she saunters off

at Lexington. Not the one with the tiger
tattoo and blow job lips, not even
the pretty one who keeps looking at you
as if your fly's open. It could be the one
reading a book, wearing head phones
and mouthing words with her eyes shut.
From here, it looks like she's reading
The Grapes Of Wrath. Under her breath
she's singing the song you first made love to,
every moan and grunt in perfect pitch.

The woman you love lives five states
away. Every weekend when the pilot
clicks off the seat belt sign, you reach
into the overhead bin and this goofy-ass,
born again grin begins to spread
across your lips and you wind up
hugging and kissing like freed hostages
and you almost forget you're forty-three
fucking years old, that this kind of thing
embarrassed you even when you were young.
You hurry to the car touching some part
of each other's body, pin her to the hood
and make out like a James Dean movie.
Getting in, she slides across the seat,
straddles your lap and you dry hump
until two half moons form on the icy
windshield and you pry your hand down
the back of her jeans seconds before
she says something about her son, fifteen
minutes, and picking him up from school.

Yes, you are in love, happier than you deserve.
You'll never have to talk to that woman,

or anybody else on the damn train, and learn
that her head's bobbing to the numbing bass
of some electronic dance track crap,
that her dog eared book is a signed copy
of Oprah's biography. No, you can consider
giving up a rent controlled apartment,
moving to Brooklyn. You can worry
about finding less and less time to write,
start to miss your closetful of porn
and wonder how difficult it will be to live
with a six year old, autistic boy
and that Linda Blair Exorcist sound
he makes whenever he gets upset.
You can remember the last time
you lived with someone, the way
you quickly tired of each other,
how the times between making love
stretched longer and wider until
you rarely touched, the way it still
hurt when she left and how for years
you believed you'd never get over it.

As you step out of the subway,
the light stings your eyes. Buds
are beginning to dot the ends
of branches and girls are wearing
barely any clothing. You walk
the few blocks to work humming
a new Brian Wilson song, remember
how much you loved summer
as a kid. When you cross the street
a car screeches to a stop.
The driver beats on his horn,
leans his head out, starts yelling

in a language you are fortunate
not to understand. You imagine
telling him you're in love,
that you can't help yourself.
You're sorry, but you don't know
what you're doing. He nods, as if
he knows too well what that means,
then drives away. But not before
bestowing on you the blessings
of a God millions believe in.

BATH TIME

His right hand
grips the safety rail.
My right hand fits
under his arm pit,
helps him step
into the tub, sit
down. His eyes shut,
lips form a tight kiss
as his ass hits
hot water. He wets
the wash cloth, reaches
in the soap dish,
lets the soap slip
through his grasp, slide
down by his feet.
He bends over,
bumps his head
on the faucet,
slurs, "Shhtt." I stop
myself from laughing,
fish for the soap,
lather up the rag,
scrub his hunched
back, bony shoulders.
I give him the wash cloth.
"Start with your arms Rob."
He rubs up and down,
moves to his neck,
chest, legs. "Don't
forget your face."
He pats his cheeks,
his chin. I grab the rag,
tell him, "Shut your eyes
tight," and wash his face.

Soap still gets in,
stings. One hand balls
into a fist, rubs
his eyes. The other
slaps the water. I get
a towel, dry his face,
say, "Stop acting
like a damn baby."
He blinks open his eyes,
mumbles, "Sorry Townry."
I muss up his hair,
"No problem, my bad,"
and point to his penis.
He strokes small circles.
We both watch it
harden, rise above
soapy water. I draw
the shower curtain,
sit on the closed
toilet lid, light
a cigarette.
        Finished,
Robert's hand rattles
the plastic curtain. I stand,
slide it open. His eyes
stare straight ahead.
I hold the tube of shampoo,
watch the green gel
squeeze into my palm,
become white foam
as my fingers spread it
through his hair. I turn
on the shower, test

the temperature, aim
the hand held nozzle,
rinse his body clean.
Water swirls down
the drain. I help him
get up, step out
of the tub. I open
a bath towel, wrap it
around his waist.
He places his hands
on my shoulders. Heat
rises off his skin, fills
the space between us.

IN THE BUILDING

The group home is getting dressed
for Halloween and Harry's picked
the shiny white Elvis jump suit.
It's way too tight. Two counselors
struggle to pull the top over
his shoulders, finally fit his arms
into sleeves. His stomach sticks
out like he's ten months pregnant
and the workers try not to laugh.
Harry wants to know whether
he can eat five slices of pizza
at the party as he struts
toward the mirror, announces
that he looks like a fucking
dickhead. I nod, tell him
he sure does, ask if he prefers
the Humpty Dumpty costume.
He pauses, curls his top lip
like the King, strums an imaginary
guitar and sings I Can't Help
Falling In Love as the workers
slow dance across the floor.

ALL THE DAYS IN THE WORLD

Everyday's an equation
complicated by fractions
and decimals that we try
to solve for X and Y except
there are no answers scraped
on a blackboard. Several times
an hour we decide how long,
how hard to fight and fit
Jesse into the world, how
often he can be himself
and let everybody else
adapt to him. It's a see-saw
we never step off, sixteen
waking hours of an endless
summer Saturday to fill.

How late can we lie
in bed as Jesse watches
the same twenty seconds
of his Winnie The Pooh
video, jumps up and down
every time the honey spills?
How long before the guy
downstairs starts beating
a broomstick against his ceiling,
bangs on our door with his fist?
Should I explain autism once
more, show him the thick rug,
the gym mats placed in front
of the TV? Should I skip
the formalities, threaten
to kick his ass again? How
often can he call the cops?

OK. It's my turn to get up.
7:15, breakfast. If you
were me, would you give
Jesse the only thing
he eats, open a new bag
of Extra Spicy Dorito Chips,
place it on the kitchen
counter, let him take
as many as he wants
whenever he wants?
How many hours would
you let him cry, howl?
Could you hold out until
Jesse grew hungry enough
to sit at the table, use
a fork to lift a sliver of egg,
bring a spoon of cereal
to his mouth, just to spit it
out and scream in pain
as if the texture, the taste
burned rivets in his tongue?

Helen walks into the kitchen
looking sleepy and soft.
I want to spend the entire
day in bed, only getting
up to change records
on the stereo. She holds
me from behind, kisses
my neck, then crouches,
grabs Jesse in a huge
mama bear hug. He wraps
his legs around her waist
and they dance over

to the couch, collapse
in bundled up laughter.

Today it's Coney Island.
The knapsack's packed
with juice and chips, sun
screen he'll immediately
wipe off. We're following
our magic rule of three
for anything new. First trip,
we drove all the way there,
slowly circled the avenues
and pointed out various
attractions and drove
right home. Second time,
we parked. Hoping to avoid
his drops to the ground
when he rolls around,
cries and refuses to move,
we plopped Jesse in
his wheelchair, took turns
pushing him, stopped
and watched the things
we expected, guessed
would light up his eyes.

This Saturday, we get out
of the car, walk hand
in hand with Jesse
in the middle. We start
with the rides, pass by
the ones with long lines
and try the Wonder Wheel.

Jesse starts out clinging
tightly in the corner
to his mom, but suspended
at the top he looks over
the edge, watches the world
below. Sliding off, he grabs
my arm and we ride five
more times. He stamps
his feet, starts to screech
when we stop in front
of the other rides. Down
the boardwalk, we pay
and enter the Aquarium.
He rushes by the walruses
and sharks we point out,
focuses on kicking pebbles
down heat grates, dropping
handfuls of food into the turtle
pool, fascinated by the way
it filters through his fingers,
kisses the surface then sinks
in slow motion. We keep
walking to the nearly deserted
beach. Jesse runs toward
the water, splashes and jumps
backwards over knee high
waves as Helen spreads
a blanket. She lays her head
in my lap, reads. I keep watch.
When it grows too dark to see
and a chilly breeze begins
to blow off the ocean, I stand
and shout, like a blue-eyed soul

singer, something about
going home. But Jesse
is too busy having a good time
to hear and I strip down
to boxers, run in, finally
catch up to him. I throw him
over my shoulder, let him kick,
scream all the way to the car.

CROSSING

Larry turned eighteen
in May. He knows
what red and green mean,
walks to the corner
and looks both ways.
Today, he's on his own
for the first time.
He walks out the door.
I count to thirty, follow.
Hidden behind the stoop,
I watch him. Head down,
hands deep in pockets,
he drags his feet,
twirls on one foot
every twenty steps,
then bends and pulls up
his socks. He turns
the corner. I run down
the block, duck behind
a black Cadillac.
When he reaches the curb,
I sneak closer, crouch
in the hardware store's
doorway. Larry lifts
his head, sees a red
light. His lips quiver,
right hand karate chops
his open left palm.
I recognize the sign
for stop, whisper
"Good." Larry looks up
and the light's green.
His right fist winds
around his clenched left

hand, tells him to walk.
He checks for cars, half
runs across Bergen Street.
Safe, Larry pirouettes
and faces me. He bows
at the waist, straightens
up, yells "Okay Tony"
and laughs out loud.

TRAINING

It's too early on a Tuesday
morning. The agency's having
budget problems, they're cutting
back on juice and fruit and the only
things on the table are coffee and tea,
bagels cut in half. The director
of our useless human resources
department is introducing the new
director of training. He's wearing
a sports jacket, a brightly striped
wide tie. His smile is too big,
he's talking too fast and he moves
around the room like Jerry Springer
on cocaine. Joseph comes from New
Hampshire and he's of course
way too young to know anything
about anything that matters.

I'm trying to pretend I'm interested
in what he's saying about seeing
the field and our consumers–yeah
that's what we call them now–
in a whole new way. He wants
to give all group home managers
a context and races through a reader's
digest version of the way society
has viewed them throughout history:
from being expelled in the dark
ages to benevolence and Christian
pity; to guinea pigs, Geraldo Rivera
and Willowbrook where half
of my guys spent their early years;
all the way to today with community
inclusion and fantasies of normalcy.

He names causes, lists diagnoses,
asks for typical characteristics.

I know all this and none of it
has helped me or the six men
in my group home. Lee still never
wants to spend time with anyone,
Larry wears the same sweatshirt
every day and James still traces
endless circles. No matter how or why
they're here, whether I call them
consumers, clients, or shake my head
when they do another nutty thing
and the thought, 'crazy ass retard',
flashes through my brain, I know
they're a lot like me and it's my job
to help make their world happier,
a bit bigger, day after day, and I wish
this guy would shut up so I can grab
a bite to eat and go do my job.

JUST ONCE

Before I shut off all
the lights and lie down
next to the already
sleeping Helen, I walk
into Jesse's room, watch
him sleep and breathe.
Such a beautiful boy,
arms and legs splayed
all over the place, covers
a tangled mess. Sometimes,
I'm tempted to bend,
kiss his cheek or forehead
and then I remember
last week, up all night,
every night, as he paced
from bedroom to kitchen
and howled for chicken
fingers, a ride to a far
away gas station to watch
his favorite blue drink
drop down a vending
machine so he could
take one sip and pour
the rest out the car window.
So, I whisper hopeful
words, almost a prayer,
that he'll sleep till morning.

I take my clothes off, pull
back the comforter,
curl close to Helen. Too
tired to sleep, I try
not to think about the last
time I worked on a poem,

the last time we made love.
I'm tired of racing home
from work to replace
the baby sitter, keep
Jesse busy and happy,
battling to cure his autism
with every breath. Please
don't let the phone ring.
I don't want to hear Helen
saying she'll be home
late again from work
helping the homeless
instead of me, resentful
she has to bring dinner
home in a bag, last night's
dishes still in the dirty
sink. I don't want to talk
about Jesse's day
or hear any complaints
about her job, his school,
Brooklyn, or terrorists
building bigger bombs,
how we should move
to Maine. Not one
word of how little
I'm doing to help her.
Just once, I want to sit
at the table, eat steak,
a baked potato. Then
I want to watch the Yankees
beat the Diamondbacks
while she cleans the kitchen,
sings Jesse to sleep, drops

her head in my lap as I pull
back her hair in my fist
and she gives me
the best blow job
in World Series history.

BASEBALL

Yes, I was one of those kids
constantly throwing a ball
against a garage door
trying to hit the corners
of the chalk drawn strike zone
while everyone else finished
chores and studied or watched
sitcoms, played with guns
and armies of tin soldiers. High
kicking like Juan Marichal,
I could hear Bob Sheppard's
benevolent thunder of a voice
announcing my name as I kicked
the rosin bag, held my hat over
my heart while the anthem
played on opening day.

My mother cut out, pinned
the tiny Long Island Press
clipping on the refrigerator
about winning the MVP
for hitting three doubles
in my first Little League
All Star game and later
called the editor to complain
about misspelling my name.
My father stopped and told
everyone he knew how I no hit
St. Kevin's, the rich kids' parish,
in the CYO championship game.

I even imagined giving up
the game winning home run
in the World Series, sitting

in front of my locker, a white
towel tightly wrapping ice
around my right arm as reporters
milled closer with note pads
and microphones. Answering
question after question with grace
and dignity, I took all the blame,
said he hit my best pitch
and with the grace of God,
promised to be back,
try to do better next year.

But no, I never thought
about being a pinch runner,
a mop up reliever or late inning
utility infielder inserted
for defense and dropping
an easy shallow pop up
or letting a routine grounder
roll through my legs
as the winning runs cross
home plate. The other team
pouring out of their dug out
like a tidal wave of champagne
while I gaze numbly into space.
Maybe my team's star player,
say Derek Jeter, would walk
over, lean in and whisper
quick assurances, condolences
as if we were at the wake
of an old schoolyard friend
while all I wanted to do is get
down on my knees, pray
that the ground would rise
and swallow me whole.

44

BLACK AND WHITE

I sometimes took the F train
home from work with Lois
and could feel her cringe
anytime a smelly black beggar
stepped in front of us, held
out his hand and god blessed us
even when we never gave them
a penny. She'd shake her head
and her black face would grimace
anytime a gaggle of teenagers
took over our car; the girls
clacking gum, swinging their fat
ghetto earrings and the boys
swaggering around in those baggy,
low riding jeans and showing off
their funky ass underwear, saying
fuck this and nigger that. She'd lean
over, grab my forearm and whisper
how she'd like to take a switch
to every one of their mothers
while wishing she had the guts
to tell them to stop acting
the fool and disgracing her.

Mondays, we'd talk about weekends.
Hers were a visiting nurse job,
a long hot bath, candles, wine,
some long time lover she'd toss
out before she left for church.
Mine was a movie or concert,
an old girl friend back in town,
dinner with a new woman, hardly
better than being alone writing.
Sundays, I'd sometimes visit

my mom and someone, my brother,
my sister or my cousin the cop
would slip in the word nigger
somewhere between the pasta and meat
about some spoiled selfish athlete,
our ruined old Brooklyn neighborhood
or welfare and Sharpton and fatherless
children and I'd keep eating, never
saying a word except to please pass
the lasagna, knowing I couldn't
change anybody's mind and trying
to believe that nothing they said
had anything to do with me.

BROOKLYN BOUND

She braces her body
between closing subway
doors, asks if this F train
goes to Coney Island.
She rushes in, pulling
the hand of a little girl
who in fifteen years
will be even prettier
than her mother. I go
back to my book, glance
at them each time
I turn the page. If
I catch the woman's eye,
I'll lift my head
at the end of every
paragraph. If she smiles,
it's after every sentence.
If she starts a conversation,
I'll smack the book shut,
throw it out the window.
But only the girl
knows I'm alive.

She looks at me
then quickly turns away.
She whips her head
around, looks back
with her mouth wide
open. Then she does it
again. This time, she
sticks her tongue out,
wags it side to side.
Finally, I get it.
Peek-A-Boo. I close,

open my eyes, act
surprised, press my nose
into a pig's snout, pull
back my hair and flap
my ears like a fat bird
taking flight. She slides
down her seat, kicking
her feet and giggling.

The woman grabs her daughter's
arm, leans over, threatens
her with a finger held
close to her face. The girl
bites her lip, sits up
and folds her hands
like an honor student
in Catholic School.
I want to apologize,
explain it was all my fault;
but I am afraid of her too.
So I read my book
as if it is getting good.
Minutes later, the train
rises out of the ground.
Sunday morning sun
lightens up the car, brightens
the neighborhoods we rattle past.
The girl climbs on her knees,
looks out the window,
points and tells her mother
about backyard swimming pools,
a nun clanging a church bell,
a man and woman slow dancing
on a fire escape. But her mind

is somewhere else—maybe
she's telling her husband
she doesn't love him anymore,
maybe she's in the shower, touching
the tiny lump on her breast—
and she stares straight ahead.

The girl keeps pointing,
slapping the window and bobbing
her head up and down, nudging
her mother's shoulder, yelling
Mommy   Mommy   Mommy
when she just gives up
kicks her mother
with both feet. Mommy
grabs her by the legs,
swings her across her lap
and whacks her ass
   —You little bitch—
five, ten, fifteen times
until the girl's bare thighs
are stained with red
burning hands and I want
to dart across the car,
somehow make her stop.

I could rub her back
as she cuddles her daughter
and they cry together.
I could sit, listen
to the woman's apologies,
say I understand. I could
tell her about the group home,
the night I hit

the retarded kid
when he bit my wrist.
How I wrote in the log
that Jimmy Hock fell
stepping out of the tub,
banged his forehead.
How the left side of his face
puffed up and turned colors
like he lost a schoolyard fight.
How I couldn't sleep
even after everyone seemed
to believe me and I kept
my job. How Jimmy
still runs to hug me
when I punch my card
nine o'clock sharp
Monday through Friday.

But all I do is hide
my eyes in the book,
hope that it's over soon,
that the next stop
is mine. The woman smoothes
her skirt flat. The girl
cries quietly, covers
her face with her hands,
her skin still pink.
When the conductor announces
Kings Highway, I get up,
wait by the door. I can feel
the girl's eyes, two snipers,
peeking between her fingers,
shooting holes in the back
of my head.

GRAVEYARD SHIFT

He leans back
in his leather lounge chair,
drinks a cold Michelob, aims
the remote at the T.V.
Click. Channel 16.
The Knicks-Sixers game.
Nothing but a bunch of monkeys
jumping up and down the court.
He flicks the switch.
Channel 7. Eye Witness News
shows a march through Bensonhurst.
Whites line the streets, spit
watermelon seeds, chant

NIGGERS GO HOME
NIGGERS GO HOME

His fingers find the beat, drum
the arm rest in time. Al Sharpton
steps to the microphone, starts
to speak.
        He grits his teeth,
mumbles, "Shut the fuck up"
and squeezes the OFF button.
The screen flashes gray, swallows
that fat black face in one big gulp.
He finishes his beer, goes
upstairs to shower, and comes down
smelling of Brut, dressed in blue.
Strapping a belt around his waist,
he places the .38 in its holster,
picks up his night stick,
walks out the door.

NUMBER 32

Today I am taking the A Train
away from Duke Ellington's
Harlem and into East New York,
Brooklyn. This beautiful tall blonde
and I are the only two Caucasians
in the crowded car. With each stop,
we move closer, pulled
together by some unnamed force.
We both know not to look
at anyone too long and even
when I make eye contact
with her, I pause for less
than a second before rushing
to read advertisements for laser
surgery. I am not scared,
not worried, just incredibly aware
of how white, like a bleached
sheet drying on a line, I feel.
I want to lean closer, whisper
in a cool, irresistible way
for her to come to my place
so we can hurry up and start
making some more of us.
When the train eases into
the next station, the doors slide
open and this young, buffed,
light skin, black man, struts
onto the train wearing
a Buffalo Bills number 32
Simpson jersey, and I want
to know what it means
to him and everyone else.
Is it sweep right, OJ gliding
behind Reggie McKenzie,

piling up 2000 yards? OJ
hurtling suitcases in crowded
airports for Hertz, guest
starring on the Love Boat?

This guy in the jersey must
remember that slow motion
car chase interrupting the Knicks
playoff game? OJ's murdered
white ex-wife and the white guy
who drove her home? Johnny
Cochrane? Me, I was working
at the group home, the only
white person on the payroll
with people I still call friends
when the not guilty verdict
was announced. I watched
Jean fall to her knees, thank
Jesus as her arms reached
for the ceiling. Annette twirled
in a circle clapping so hard
that sparks of sweat shot out.
The two men shook hands.
I wasn't quite sure why,
but I realized it was a time
when we couldn't say anything
to each other. I walked outside,
sat on the stoop and waited
for yellow buses to bring
our boys home from school.
Back on the subway that guy
is talking to the woman, jotting
numbers on a scrap of paper

and she's smiling, touching
her pretty blonde hair, folding
the paper in her jacket pocket.
Maybe she will call him tomorrow.
They can go for drinks or dinner
or dancing. Maybe they will fall
in love, spend their honeymoon
searching for the real killers.

THE LAST TIME I USED THE N WORD

Was back in the New York City crack years,
a perfectly crisp fall day, climbing out
of the F train hole and walking the block
and a half to the group home, decades
before Brooklyn grew too cool for its own
good. I nodded to old man Jose as he hung
flower pots from the awning of his store.
My hands were tucked in my pockets
and Van Morrison's Full Force Gale
was blowing through my head when a kid
started walking next to me and said
almost in a whisper 'mister give me
your wallet.' I lifted my hands, looked
him up and down, a thin brown skinned,
maybe thirteen year old kid and I smirked,
kept walking when another kid grabbed
my other shoulder, said 'we ain't shittin''
and pressed this tiny gun against my neck.
I just raised my arms to god on high
and surrendered as he dug deep
in my pockets until Jose yelled
something in Spanish and they tore
ass through the schoolyard, down
into the projects. I waved to Jose
and walked up the steps to my job,
rang the bell and Liz, who told everyone
that she was my black mama, asked
'child, what happened to you'
and wrapped me in her huge arms
saying those fucking niggers
and I mumbled mostly to myself,
'yeah, those fucking niggers'
as if I was singing along to the radio
and the word felt so right, so good,
rolling, tumbling out of my mouth.

ON THE SEVENTH DAY

When God is leaning back,
all full of himself, and resting
on his laurels, I get up early,
go to my desk and try to take
his place, fill a few blank pages,
create my own world. Maybe
Monk's Bright Mississippi
or Ahmad Jamal plays
in the background
as the characters doo wop
and stutter weave, in
and out, between, the lines:
a twenty-one year old
autistic boy, learning
to be on his own, bites
his wrist and slams
his head on the floor
and still can't tell me why,
my mom calls and we hardly
ever have much to say
except a cousin I never met
died of cancer yesterday,
a day before his 30th birthday,
and she wants me to buy a card,
write a hundred dollar check
to help pay for the plot, and yes
my heart is still slowly healing
from this summer's surgery
and the load of loneliness
that has always surrounded me
feels heavier as I struggle
to imagine what a good day
could ever be like again.

And when I take a breath
step out of my head,
I read about one more
young black man, his hair
freshly braided, walking
down another unlit
stairway with his girlfriend
in Brooklyn's Pink Houses
as a rookie cop patrols
the hallway toward him,
his gun unholstered, and opens
a door. I want to go back
to my desk and pretend
I'm God so I can write
how the bullet whizzes
past, ricochets harmlessly
to the floor since God
chose to sit idly by, act
like he had little to do
with any of it, content to speak
through some Sunday morning
preacher about a better place,
that the lord never gives more
than his children can bear,
how we will one day understand
his master plan when just once
I want God to stand up, shine
beacons of the brightest light
and share the shame and blame
while the wide world cries
with its head in its hands.

MIME

Sunday, the clown picked you
out of the crowd for a game
of tennis played in mime.
Standing twenty feet away,
his serving motion started
the match. The crowd laughed
as you chased the bouncing
ball, an ace. Next point,
you were ready. Waiting
with knees bent and rocking
rhythmically, you passed him
with a backhand down the line.
His white eyes widened,
red mouth dropped open.
He never would've guessed
that you're deaf and not dumb
at all. Head down, you toweled
off your racquet handle.
When the clown volleyed
deep and charged the net,
your perfectly placed lob
landed beyond his reach.
When the clown hit one
behind his back, your return
was a shot between your legs.
Match point, you reached back
for your hardest serve. The clown
caught the ball in his mouth,
tumbled in a backwards somersault
and landed in a cross-legged
sitting position. You threw
your racquet in the air, danced
a quick six step shuffle
and vaulted over the net.

While you two shook hands,
the clown leaned over,
whispered, "Shit, how'd
you get so good?"

EASTER

I'm up early folding the mattress
back into the couch. Helen is asleep
behind our closed bedroom door.
My stepson is sliding the first
of today's maybe two hundred videos
into the machine's slot. Even though
no one in this apartment has any reason
to believe in Jesus, last night
we pretended everything was good.
Jesse wasn't autistic and Helen
wasn't falling out of love with me.
We sat at the kitchen table, dipped
hard boiled eggs into plastic cups
filled with colored water. Jesse
crouched, his eyes level with the edge
of the table as he jumped in delight
every time we dunked an egg
beneath the surface. Helen
caught my eye a few times
and neither one of us could keep
from smiling. When Jesse lost
interest, walked back to his room,
we finished the dozen, hardly
talking. She then said goodnight,
took a book to bed while I played
the radio softly, thought about
how hopeless I felt as I bent
down, hid a purple egg under
the bed, leaned over to kiss Jesse
while he slept so perfectly.

VISITOR'S DAY AT THE GROUP HOME

Robert, twenty-one yesterday,
walks down stairs carefully.
Both hands clench rails. Head
down, he watches each foot land.
Reaching bottom, he claps twice,
sees her and smiles. He mumbles
and she knows he's saying mommy.
She hugs him close. Drool slides
down the back of her neck. "Mommy
missed Robert so much." He digs
into the shopping bag of gifts,
finds a Walkman. She clamps
the headphones on him. He bobs
like a spastic puppet to the Temptations'
Greatest Hits. She opens a pint
of rice pudding, starts to spoon it
into his mouth. I pass her a handful
of napkins. Later, she lays his head
in her lap, sings Happy Birthday
and lights matchsticks to wish on.
I place a coloring book, his special
extra thick crayons on the table.
He scribbles interlocking spirals
while his eyes track her movements.
A car horn sounds and she steps
to the window, motions 'just
a moment' with her hand.
She bends, kisses Robert's
forehead. "See you next week
sweetheart." We nod goodbye
as she pushes open the door.
Robert throws a blue crayon
across the room, crumples
his drawing. He stands,
climbs up the stairs and fits
into his bed, his clothes still on.

VISITS

Days like this I wish
I was six years old
and autistic, like Jesse,
the way he opens the door
and grabs my hand,
leads me to his room
on my weekly visits.
His mother stands by
a window, her arms
crossed loosely against
her chest, thinking
I guess. He stands on
this special, worn out circle
of rug, says, "One, two, three,
up Tony" and I lift him,
throw him high as I can.
He lands on the bed
laughing, and I pounce
on top of him, lie there
until he wraps his arms
around my neck and I ask,
no beg, for just one squeeze,
and he pulls me tighter,
hugs me for less than
an instant. We do this
over and over, both of us
running out of breath, seven,
ten minutes, until he says,
"See you later," walks me
down the hall to the room
where I used to sleep.

If I paid the Spanish lady
with the tiny barking dog
who lives down the hall

to come by once or twice
a week, showed her how
to pick Jesse up, throw
him on the bed exactly
the way I do, I'm not sure
he could tell the difference.
And if I was Jesse
I wouldn't love Helen
so desperately. Anyone
could take her place:
The tall, pretty teacher
who lives in Jersey, loves
Lucinda Williams, poetry,
Southside Johnny, driving
fast and dancing slow.
The thirty-three year old
with her dark eyes and sexy
mouth, the Thurman Munson
baseball card taped
to her bedroom mirror.
The woman sitting across
the table at my best friend's
wedding. Last weekend,
alone in Baltimore. Someone
said her name was Jackie.
She had this little girl
voice and kept leaning
over as she bit
into soft shell crabs.

GOODBYE

Today, I picked Jesse up
from music group. He said
my name soon as I stepped
through the door, tried to run
to me. The therapist stood
in his way, forced him to stay
until he made eye contact,
said goodbye to her assistant,
the other kids. She slowly
walked him over to me,
assured me how much better
he was doing while he tugged
on my arm repeating 'home'
louder and louder. I thanked her
while we headed out the door,
tried to keep him from jumping
into every puddle, steer him
from bumping into people
as we turned down subway stairs.

Jesse took a window seat,
got on his knees and traced
the outline of his face as we rode.
I finger counted the six stops
to Hamilton Parkway, promised
that his mom would be waiting
for him. When the train rose
out of the ground, climbed up
into the cloudless sky, he ran
to the front door. I stood behind
him, played with his hair as all
of Red Hook spread beneath us.
I glanced at the other riders,
curious whether they could tell

something was wrong with Jesse
then wondered what he was thinking,
if his brain could hold anything
other than shapes and colors
flying past, the feel of glass
against his fingertips, the thought
that his mommy would be waiting
three, now two, stations away.
I imagined what he would do
if we stayed on longer, rode out
to Coney Island. Would he stop
crying and fighting long enough
to see or hear, smell, the ocean?
Would he run across the sand
like the summer before, strip
down to his shorts? Jump
and play in the waves until
the last light leaves the sky?

The closets are empty
and piles of packed boxes
line the walls of his house,
but I'm not sure Jesse knows
that this means he's moving
back to Maine in the morning.
I don't know if he can grasp
the concept of missing someone
or understand how hard
it is for me to keep from crying.
He has no idea that I met him
three years ago. I went
with Helen to pick him up
from school one afternoon.

The Sunday after, finished
with my bowl of oatmeal,
I was watching her lift
her teacup to her lips
when I realized I wanted
to spend my life with her
and it scared me to death.

I don't know what Jesse
remembers about Maine,
about moving to Brooklyn;
if he knows when things started
to fall apart or why me and his mom
couldn't find a way to stay together;
if he remembers that I moved
down the block, kept visiting him
while everyone I know told me
to let go and move on,
that I didn't owe him a thing,
and no one seemed to accept
or understand I love Jesse,
that the way he will never fit
in the world reminds me of me
and I wish he was my son,
my eight year old boy.
My, my, mine.

FAITH

You find it hard to believe
in any kind of God: Priests,
little boys, countless kept secrets;
Israelis, Palestinians, that dirty war
over somebody's idea of holy land;

Your girlfriend's autistic son,
and how she stopped loving you
suddenly; the sharp, numbing
loneliness. Yet, every morning

You reach across the mattress
quiet that bleating alarm,
sit up, still half asleep,
ready to do whatever
the hell it is you now do.

AFTER

It's the night after Christmas
and it's snowing in Brooklyn
again. The wind's blowing
harder and flakes are falling
faster than they did 8 years ago.
This time, my phone won't ring
in the cold cold night, your soft
sleepy voice won't tempt me
into walking through Kensington,
the only two people sweeping
snow off car hoods, throwing
snow balls as your hair grew
all wet and tangled. No, we won't
remove our boots in the hall,
sit on the couch kissing
tentatively, make our way
to the bed for the first time.

But if I was tempted to pick
up the phone, I wonder how
long it would take you to recognize
my voice? Would you know me
in one, two, five syllables
and win the grand prize
chosen especially for you?
Would you remember me at all,
the way you'd walk your dogs
late at night and call hoping
to hear something sweet
and sarcastic before you fell
asleep next to your boyfriend?
If I asked you to go walking,
yes tonight, how many breaths
before you'd recover your

frazzled grace and tell me
it's too late, too far, to walk
from Austin to Brooklyn?

Is your husband home, down
in the basement, playing
with computers and machines
making music without melodies
or words? I know, I know
you still love Bill. Would you tell me
in a rushed whisper not to call
ever again, click off quickly?
Would you wish me a merry
Christmas, move to another
room, close the door behind
you? Clutch your new daughter
closer, carry her with you
or lay her down in her crib
quietly? Could I forgive you
if you had a Texas accent?
Would it possibly lend
your words a softer sexier
slur, or make them sound
too sweet and too fake?

Would you ask about my writing,
tell me how much you loved
my new book, how the poems
still tear you apart, make you
cry when you read them
late at night and pretend
you're not the woman
in the ones that hurt the most?

Would you ask about Jesse?
Would your hands move
like giddy fish as you go on
and on about your baby girl?
Could I imagine how deeply
the light in your eyes burns
when you tell me her name?

Would you say something,
anything about how you miss
New York City, how often
you think of me, no matter
how much you want to forget
those three years? Would you
tell the truth or lie, say
you really loved me?
How you hope I'm happy
and I've learnt to let go,
that this new year
will be my best ever
when we say goodbye
one more time?

FIVE YEARS LATER

My brother was on his way
to a dental appointment
when the second plane hit
four stories below the office
where he worked. He's never
said anything about the guy
who took football bets, how
he liked to watch his secretary
walk, the friends he ate lunch with,
all the funerals. Maybe, shamed
by his luck, he keeps quiet,
afraid someone might guess
how good he feels, breathing.

PHYSICS

This morning, the narrator
of the book I'm reading
is trying to fall asleep listening
to a tape on physics. A crisp
scientific voice is explaining
there's no such thing as the past,
that each moment exists forever
caught in a stringy tangle of light
and mass and I remember
this woman I hardly knew
telling me she lost her virginity
and finalized her third divorce
the same date the atom bomb,
code named Little Boy,
was dropped on Hiroshima
killing more than 155,000 people.
August sixth, 1945. Louis Armstrong
died that day in 1971 and in 1948
a freak heat wave off the coast
of Central Portugal pushed
temperatures up to 158° for two
minutes. Wouldn't It Be Nice
was a top ten hit that week
in 1966, the summer I kissed
a girl and felt my first t-shirt
covered tit playing Seven Minutes
In Heaven with Geraldine Quinn
while my friends stood outside
counting down the seconds.

I thought about a Saturday
in that same summer. My team
beats St. Kevin's rich kids, wins
the 8th Grade, CYO championship.
The girl I like sits in the stands,

her hair wrapped high in curlers
as I strike out the last guy
with an inside fastball. I punch
my fist in my mitt, hug
John Calamari my catcher
and roll on the ground
with everybody else in a jumble
of joy. I'm sitting on
the bench, untying my spikes
and my dad leans down,
"Three for four and a no-hitter,
that's what you're supposed
to do, all damn time." He smiles,
slaps the bill of my hat.

Later, at around 7:15 or so
I realize it's the anniversary
of the day my father died.
I call my mom and both
of us find it hard to believe
eight years have already passed.
Always, I want Mickey Mantle
to be chasing down fly balls
in Yankee Stadium, Thurman
Munson lining a two out double
into the gap and tying the score,
Jeter making that back hand flip
against Oakland over and over.

Somehow, it's always the night
after Christmas. Snow falls
in fat sexy flakes. Suzanne
walks over, sits on my couch
and plays with her scarf, says

she doesn't know why she's here,
she really loves her boyfriend.
I've never done anything
like this before either. Usually,
I'm slow and awkward,
but I start kissing her
like I know what I'm doing
and she kisses me back softer
and deeper and walks through
the kitchen and into my bedroom
then comes back the next night
and both of us start to fall in love.

And tonight, when I turn out
the lights and pile the covers
high around my head, I wish
that physicist was singing me
to sleep, a sweet rhyming lullaby
in angelic Brian Wilson harmony,
telling me all about another
woman I love, her son's
big green, owl-shaped clock
sitting on his dresser and how
he keeps it set to the same time
no matter how many nights
I sneak in while he's sleeping
and move the owl's wings.
It's 3:12 again.
His mom has his arms
and I have a hold of his legs.
We're swinging Jesse, higher
and higher until he nearly
scrapes the ceiling. We let go
and he is flying, suspended over
his big soft bed and laughing.

RENAL SONOGRAM

Tuesday morning and I'm lifting
my shirt, lying on my back
in a dark room. I have trouble
with the lab technician's accent,
ask her to repeat every question
as she spreads gel on my belly,
presses a wand here and there
taking pictures of my kidneys.

"Please, deep breath." Holding it,
I am hoping for easy answers,
a pill, less sodium in my diet
to stop my calves from swelling
as I sit at my desk writing,
standing and yelling for more
at Los Lobos' Sunday night show.

"No breathing please." I think
about this morning's email, news
that my oldest friend's nephew
is dead. Thirty-eight-years old,
he went to grammar school
with my baby brother. The police
suspect foul play and Kevin's
driving all the way from Cleveland
with his second wife. The wake
will either be a crying, moaning
mess or a half empty room filled
with awkward guilty silence
and I wish I didn't have to go.
"Turn on side, please. Face wall."

After this, I'll ride the G train
to the group home, fire the guy
I was training to help cut

my work load in half. I feel
bad. He's twenty-six, a funny,
ambitious kid who needs money
for his "baby mama drama."
But his attention span's shorter
than a Facebook message
and he kept borrowing cash
from the workers he supervised.

"Lie on back one time again.
Lower pants please." I undo
my belt, slide my pants down
so the top of my pubic hair
shows. "Hold breath please now."
Younger, I'd have to concentrate,
try hard not to get an erection.
Now, I would be pleased to feel
my cock growing uncontrollably.

I watch the technician carefully
as she ignores me, does her job.
I imagine her hair let loose
from her bun, the lab coat falling
to the floor. But no, she's not
the kind of woman I can picture
working in a Chinatown spa
leading me to the back room.

"Relax. All done, please." I leave
knowing I will have to wait
patiently as possible until next
Tuesday, 12:45, for my doctor
to interpret the results, maybe
look me in the eye and deliver
news I'd never want to hear
or the chance of a happy ending.

LARGER THAN LIFE

I haven't watched a minute
of this winter's Olympics, carefully
avoided all the flag waving, all the medal
counting. I missed the sublime skaters
and merely glanced at the headline
announcing that a Georgian luge athlete
died on a first day practice run. But I remember
that long ago summer when the gymnasts
were all thirteen and built like muscular twigs,
their bright white teeth fixed in graceless
smiles, the anointed crowd favorite,
her Stalinesque coach and her father
dying of cancer back home in Kansas.

With background strings swelling,
the announcer's reverent voice
told us about her long endless hours
of dedicated day after day training
and how she spent the last four years,
really her entire life, for this one moment.
She raised her hands high above her head
and bounded, bounced, danced, jumped,
twirled, flipped, and oh shit, slipped,
skidded and crumbled into a heap.
The crowd hushed and I couldn't keep
myself from hoping she'd pick herself
slowly up, bravely finish her program.

Or better yet, get up girl, c'mon, start
walking and keep walking, off the mats
and through the arena's basement, step
into the world. Go home and fall in love
with the boy next door, wear a white dress,
build an ordinary, fuller life. Maybe, a life
like mine: Scan box scores on crowded subways,

walk down tree lined Brooklyn blocks, climb
the group home's stoop, open the door to find
my second favorite kid looking like he caught
a left hook from Mike Tyson in his prime.
Then try to figure out what happened, take
steps to make sure no one hurts Lee again.

Leave work after lunch, ride the railroad out
to Long Island, visit my brother serving time
for a DUI. Sit in an over-crowded, noisy trailer
for two hours counting other white people,
the breathlessly sexy women, their restless kids.
Get screened in, watch my brother walk
across the cafeteria, shake hands, relieved
that he looks healthy, seems in good spirits.
Can I mail him anything else? Try ignoring
all the women bending and flashing breasts,
the slow soulful kisses, the three year olds'
bouncing happily, wrapping their arms
around their daddys' necks, giggling.

End the evening at a jazz club listening
to a fat black man play piano, make Elvis
sound like prayer and old river hymns
grind like mortal sin while I sit across
from a beautiful new woman wearing
polka dots and braids, eating barbecue.
Marianne moves closer and squeezes
my arm, laughs. I imagine more music,
darkly lit bars, sweaty rock n roll.
I lean in and find her mouth, fast forward
to her hallway, watch her skirt swirl, lift
lightly as we climb five steep flights, press
against her as she pushes the door open.

NIECE

Last week when my baby brother's wife
gave birth to their first child, a girl,
I was visiting my ex-girlfriend, her
twelve year old son, Jesse, in Maine.

Today, I'm standing on their Long Island steps
waiting for someone to come to the door.
My brother grabs my jacket, leads me
down the hall with this dazed half smile.

No one in my family knows how to talk
about anything that matters, but our eyes collide
and I sense we both recognize how different,
warm and charged, this piece of quiet feels.

His wife walks across the living room carrying
a too pink bundle, humming almost imperceptibly.
She's wearing gray sweats and looks tousled,
softer, more beautiful than I thought possible.

I can't tell if the baby is as pretty as my mother,
delighted to be a grandmother for the third time,
insisted over and over during our long distance call
or if she looks like anyone in anybody's family.

I nod and my brother's wife leans closer, places
the baby in my arms and I can't believe how tiny
this little girl is, how every single finger is a bigger
miracle than anything I've seen in too many years.

Riding the railroad home, I'll glide by empty apartment
buildings covered with whirling slashes of graffiti
and wonder why I never wanted anything this wonderful
to happen to me, if I'll miss it more the older I get.

I'll think about what Jesse means to me, how easy
it is to be generous, to simply love him unconditionally
from far away and whether I'd turn into myself
become a selfish, impatient, too strict father up close.

But right now, Alexis Leigh is resting in my lap
occasionally yawning and stretching, letting
the pacifier slip out of her mouth and I'm rocking
gently doing all I can to keep her happy.

THIRTEEN

Five states away, Jesse's
celebrating a birthday. All
last week he read social stories
trying to learn what cake, lit
candles, pizza party hats and gifts
are supposed to mean to him.
I play the jumpy email video,
watch as he slides into a booth,
shakes salt into his palm, tilts
his head sideways and, like always,
his eyes light up as crystals pour
from his fingers like fairy dust.
He makes his infamous shrieking
sound when the teacher hands
him a hat and he doesn't stop
screaming or pounding the table
until she stuffs it in the trash.

A few kids slide in
next to him, across from him
and take turns slapping,
grabbing his hand in different
secret ways and Jesse doesn't
start howling, doesn't try
to hide under the table or yell
for his mom's blue van.
He just covers his mouth
with his hand as he laughs
so hard that goose bumps
start to crawl down my arm.
Patiently he waits for the pizza,
blows the candles out, takes
a slice, nibbles counter clockwise
around its steaming edges,

drinks half a Snapple
and then rips his gifts open.

When I visited last winter,
he spent nearly four hours
repeating "Tony airport bye"
and I wasn't sure he knew me
until the next morning when
he placed his face close to mine.
He put his finger in his mouth,
tried to make that popping sound
I showed him the first time
we met and I remembered
how he'd jump with joy,
crumble into a soft, giggling,
rolling-across-the-floor-ball
every time I did it. He'd grab
my finger, lift it to my lips
and say "Again Tony, again."
Later, he sprawled across
my lap, let me rub his feet
as he turned pages of shiny
alphabet books, slid his fingers
over the illustrations like
he was speed reading Braille.

At thirteen, he's bigger, stronger.
He throws clothes, magazines
across his bed, desk and floor
like any teenager and he plays
his MP3 endlessly. Still
he listens to the same six
Sesame Street jingles over

and over. Recently he's pulled
hair, torn shirts, bit teachers
and attacked Helen in the middle
of the night once. She never
told me how badly he hurt her,
but she's having trouble sleeping
and feels more overwhelmed
than usual. He's started
on a low dose of medication,
but she can't tell how much
it's helping and no one knows
about long term side effects.

I want to book an early
morning flight, drive over
the hills, ride to the rescue
like John Wayne's cavalry.
I want to remember how
much I miss and love both
of them, forget the part
of me that's relieved
I no longer feel guilty
for not spending every hour
of every day trying to cure
his autism, that even if me
and his mom still loved
each other the way we swore
we would, hunkered down
close and deep in our bunkers,
there may never be a way
to make a place in this world
for Jesse or either one of us.

BIRTHDAYS

Jesse and Gillian, the daughter of my long
        distance friend, both turned
eighteen in June. She's decided to study history,
        political science at Harvard.
Her mom already misses her. Jesse graduated from his special
        program. I watched the video
my ex girlfriend emailed a few times every morning
        this week: Scenes of yoga poses,
his art exhibit at a local gallery, counselors, teachers
        and students wishing him all the luck
in the world, saying how much they'll miss him as he sat
        on a low slung hammock and a Cat
Stevens song played. He's spending the weekend at a Water
        Park and he'll start regular high school
this Fall with two workers shadowing him down
        hallways, through classrooms.

At eighteen, I was lost and living in my parents' basement,
        fighting with my father, wondering
how many years I could kill in college before I was forced
        to find a job I'd hate for the rest
of my life. I was happiest running full court and pitching
        stickball at the schoolyard, listening
to Dylan, writing in spiral notebooks, trying to find the perfect
        words to say to Julia Jordan, a place
in the world to belong. Like Jesse, like Gillian, like you. Day after
        every damn lonely, blessed day.

TWENTY-EIGHT

This woman who told me
I was too old for her
said she sometimes wonders
what I was like at 28. Sure,
I was 10-20 pounds thinner
with darker, longer hair
hanging down my back.
But already, I had started
working with retarded
and autistic kids, sending
my poems out, trying to learn
if they had anything to say
to anyone other than me.

I was always quiet, shy
and I probably thought
too much, never learned
how to let go and have fun.
I can be self-absorbed,
thoughtless, too often sarcastic,
irreverent and hard headed.
And no I never liked parties
or politics or money and most
people. I didn't play guitar,
drive a fast car, never dreamt
of spending a year in Paris,
Timbuktu or Nepal, a weekend
in the Hamptons or building
a mansion on a hill, filling it
with kids and lovable pets.

Even then, I knew that listening
to 2 minutes and 25 seconds
of Brian Wilson or driving down
a late night highway shouting

along to "Thunder Road" was as good
as I could feel, that the rhythm
of a basketball bouncing past
my Sunday morning window
or a backyard six-year-old
whacking a whiffle ball
with a plastic bat, sliding
into home plate was as close
to God as I would ever get.

But I was always good
at listening and talking
and touching, and when
I was 28, I was in love,
mad-crazy-deep-silly, radio
song, it takes two, you
and me against the world
kind of love and anytime
we sat at a table and broke
bread, spent a rainy weekend
tangled up in light blue sheets
or held hands on the crowded
Monday morning F train
stuck once again in the tunnel
between Queens and Manhattan
I was sure we'd last forever.

At 28, this girl was so in love
with me that her amazing
green-brown eyes would get
all lit up whenever she looked
at me. At 28, I had everything
in the world I ever needed.
At 28, I was just about
as dumb as I am now.

JUNE 11th

It's Sunday, a family barbecue
ending with my niece holding
her Rapunzel doll and leaning
over, helping me blow out
the candles on the Carvel cake
celebrating my birthday.
I ask for the biggest piece,
eat around the crunchy
middle part that gets bigger
every year and save the vanilla
ice cream for last. My mom
brings up my father, the year
he didn't give me a gift
when I wouldn't cut
my hair and he found out
she slipped me fifty dollars
for Beach Boys tickets,
how he didn't speak
to either one of us
until the month ended.
I remember she treated
him nicer while I pretended
not to care. Now, nearly
the same age as my father
when he died, I appreciate
how much he's missed.
He never met Helen
or my step son, never
had the chance to wonder
what went wrong or blame
me when they moved back
to Maine. He missed
my brother's marriage,
his suburban success.

He never got to see
my brother's daughter
or her baby brother
who's sitting in a high chair
across from me. Daniel
keeps dropping his spoon
and he doesn't stop
crying until he gets it back.
I can almost see my father
picking it up, taking it
to the sink and saying
"enough of this crap,"
or maybe, softer now,
he'll make a loud, silly
sound and fit the spoon
into his grandson's
pudgy excited fingers.

ALIVE ON ARRIVAL

Thirty, thirty-five years after
being called the next Dylan,
his debut album playing
on every FM radio station
and "Romeo's Tune" bulleting
up the Billboard charts, Steve
Forbert is pacing the dark stage
of a small club. He's plugging
in his own guitar, adjusting
the mic's height, strumming
a few chords and blowing
into the harmonica wired
around his neck. Almost
show time, I order an over
priced flat bread pizza instead
of the tiny Angus sliders.

Forbert opens with 'Thinkin',
a slinky shuffle tune telling us
not to spend too much time thinkin'
and thinkin' or you'll wind up
stranded behind. Tapping the table
to his easy rhythms and natural
melodies, I go down to Laurel
in his songs with him, spend
a week in January drinking
and driving with old home town
friends and end up sleeping
in his boyhood bed, listening
to church bells ring, wondering
what kind of guy I really am.

Right now, I'm a guy who thinks
I'm sick of winter. I can't seem

to shake this week long cold
and I'm not in love with anyone.
I'm sitting across from Rob
who's sipping whiskey trying
to forget he lost his keys today,
that it cost two hundred dollars
to change the locks. My ex
in Maine has been angry
since she found out I put
her name in my last book
of poems. We're not speaking
and I miss her son badly.

Between songs, the audience
can't help yelling out requests.
I resist the temptation to get
on my knees, beg for "I Blinked
Once," "Born Too Late." Tomorrow,
Rob will be riding the C train
to Fort Greene to give things
with this young woman another
chance. I'm thinking I'll send Helen
a hand written letter, apologize
again and hope she'll forgive me.

Forbert fills ninety minutes
plus two encores with instantly
recognizable cuts we all mouth
the words to. He covers the Kinks,
Jimmie Rogers and sprinkles
in a few album obscurities,
a bunch of new tunes he's clearly
dying to play. Maybe they won't
find their way to your car radio

or download into the ears
of all those hipsters crowded
onto the late night L train
back to Williamsburg, but Forbert
seems happy enough playing
guitar and singing his songs
while we clap and yell for more.

He stands at the bar, signs
old vinyl covers, talks, laughs
and poses for photographs
as he sells old and new CDs,
finally says good night,
packs up his truck and heads
down the line to another joint.
And no, I'm not dreaming about
happy ever after true true love
or even one quiet, snow falling
fireplace evening in Helen's arms
as I climb down subway stairs.
I'm thinking about the last time
I flew into Portland, wandered
around the airport and heard
Jesse call my name. I'm thinking
I'd be happy to fall asleep
beneath a deep pile of blankets,
an electric heater at my feet
and wake up way too early
to that silly nonsense song
Jesse hums as he lies in bed,
gets ready for a new morning.

AIRPORT

I don't know what's wrong
with me, ten years later
and whenever my plane
touches down in Portland
it flares up like an old injury,
a long ago, left over ache
from the shoulder I separated
while making that diving,
game-winning catch as time
ran out. I can still feel hints
of excitement as I lift my bag,
walk down the aisle hoping,
half expecting to see Helen
on her tip toes at the gate
waving. I can almost feel
her arms around me,
my lips kissing hers.

But then I come to my senses,
remember how she suddenly
went from telling me all
her thoughts and secrets
to extended bouts of dark
icy silence, the way she once
couldn't keep her hands off
of me whenever I was near
to sleeping on the couch
while I remained the same
weird wonderful asshole
I have always been.

Today, she's too busy
with all-day office meetings
about the chronically
homeless to pick me up.
I'll eat a late breakfast,
egg whites, lightly buttered
toast at the airport, then
catch a cab to her place.
Walking slowly, aimlessly,
I move among hordes
of ex-hippies and fresh
faced students hugging
somebody they missed
desperately when I hear
someone call my name.

Jesse, almost a man,
and his respite worker
Mary stand in front of me.
He lets me squeeze him
in a sideways half hug
for nearly three seconds,
then lends me his cheek
for a quick kiss before
he grabs my bag. I follow
Jesse through revolving
glass doors, blindly cross
the parking lot, smiling
like a care free idiot.

DISNEY WORLD

John's the highest functioning guy
in the group home. He always
says hello, asks about your day,
smiles and never forgets your name
like I often will. Everybody
loves him and every Monday
he sits by my desk, tells me
about his wonderful weekend
whether he went to the movies
Friday night, spent Saturday
winning ribbons and medals
at Special Olympics, played
Coney Island Skee Ball
all Sunday afternoon or sat
on the couch staring into space
with Channel 13's pledge week
blaring in the background.

No, he's not on any medication
and no I'm not too jealous
he appears happier than me.
Maybe I should be grateful
he doesn't shit or piss his pants,
rip his shirts or throw chairs
at the ceiling like the others
and be satisfied helping him
learn to cook, cross streets,
count his money. Yet sometimes
he pisses me off with the way
he says he likes everything
exactly the same amount
and never lets anyone know
what he's thinking or feeling,
how he takes so long to answer

a question or make a simple
choice as if he's worried
or scared that anything he says
will be wrong and something
terrible will happen to him
and sometimes, I admit it,
I do imagine smacking
that sweet dumb boring smile
right off his damn mouth.

But I've tried to let John know
that this life is his and my job
is to help him live it the way
he likes, that it's okay to tell me
what he wants and doesn't want
and he doesn't need permission
to feel sad or bad or angry.
Every once in awhile I think
he's beginning to understand.
I now know he'd rather eat
McDonald's than Chinese food,
that there's no way he'll ever
get on a roller coaster or step
into a pool more than two feet
deep while wearing a life jacket
and holding a staff member's hand,
that he prefers staying home
watching Country Music Awards
over sitting in tenth row seats
as Springsteen and the E Streeters
play a benefit show. I tell myself,
it's okay, everyone has opinions
and fears, none are good or bad

and I try to pretend to believe
that bull shit when talking to John.

Still, these past few days,
John's really surprised me.
I didn't know what to say
when he told me he'd rather not
let me borrow a Johnny Cash CD
I gave him for his last birthday.
Even though I swore I'd buy him
a new one if I broke or lost it,
he shook his head no, said
if it was okay with me, he wanted
to keep the one he had. Today
when he asked about my day,
I told him I was tired and stressed
worrying about his roommate.
John hoped Joey would get well,
come home from the hospital soon.
He then paused for a moment
asked if this meant he wouldn't
be going to Disney World.
I tried to describe what it meant
to be generous and thoughtful, why
no one really likes self centered
cheap bastards. When he looked
down, took a deep breath, I thought
he might apologize. Instead, John
asked about Florida again, started
clapping when I finished explaining
about reservations, penalty fees
and packing properly for an 8:00 AM
flight out of LaGuardia next Monday.

WEATHER

When we walk out the door,
Jesse's respite worker asks him
about the weather. It's February
in Maine and there's snow
on the ground. He answers
"Clouds, wind, too cold."
Still, I have to remind him
to zip his hoodie, ask maybe
we should go back inside,
change his sandals for socks
and boots. He blurts, "No
socks, no shoes" as I dig
my hands deeper into pockets,
trot to the car. His worker
turns down the radio,
shows him his cell phone.
A list of different cities
roll down the screen,
their current temperatures
next to them. The worker
points to one and Jesse
answers what he'd wear
if he were there, a coat,
or shorts and a tee shirt.
When the worker points
to another, Jesse pauses,
then says, "New York, Tony
house" and I wonder whether
he remembers that eight hour
U Haul drive when he moved
to Brooklyn the summer me
and his mom were in love.

Jesse, five and a half years old,
incessantly sweating and still

marching obsessively room
to room closing every window
tight; sitting on my lap, licking
the burnt orange remnants
of Extra Spicy Doritos off
his fingers as I talk on
the phone; subwaying
to the end of the F line
and jumping Coney Island
waves as it grows too dark
to see, playing Rosalita,
We're Having A Party,
A Good Feelin' To Know
on the stereo, blasting them
in the same exact order
anytime his mom called
to say sorry she'd be home
late again from work
as I lift him as high
as the ceiling, bounce
him on the bed over
and over until we both
run out of breath, ready
for a Beach Boys lullaby
to close our eyes, hopefully
help him, me, sleep
through the night, please.

APPLIED BEHAVIOR ANALYSIS

Every few minutes or so,
Jesse earns a point for calm
hands, calm body and a quiet
voice. Mary, today's worker,
reaches out and Jess clicks
the counter in her hand.
Whenever he's fidgety, loud
or perseverates they stop, wait
for him to become quiet, calm
again. His worker constantly
stays with him and carries
a clipboard with his schedule
printed on it. 10:00, walk
to Shaw's super market
with Mary, buy one drink.
Soon as he pays the cashier,
Jesse says, 'cross out please'
over and over until Mary
finds her pen and draws
a line through that section
of the schedule. He seems
happier watching his worker
cross out the words describing
his just finished activity
than spending hours on water
slides and roller coasters.

Back home, he takes a break
for eight minutes. 10:28,
means a half hour of table
work. He finds and circles
words from rows of jumbled
letters, reads news articles
or plays Blink. 11:09, drive

to the gym, work out on five
machines three times each,
then yoga, hot tub. 12:16,
Mobil gas station, buy drink
and snack. 12:34, drive to lake,
throw rocks, watch the ripples
disappear. Intermittingly,
the worker asks if Jesse
wants to cash in his points
for a five minute break, music
in the car or another drink.
Jesse says, "Yes, please."

In between activities,
they stop and talk. "Jesse,
what did we just do?" Who
went to the lake with you?"
When Jesse responds
with a word, a phrase,
a nodding head or finger
flapping she says, "Full
sentence please." Sometimes,
she writes the answer
down, tells him to read it
slowly, clearly. "I went
to the lake to throw rocks
with Mary." He recites it
like a robotic operator
who can never tell you
what you really want
to know. "Jesse, what
does it feel like to be you."
"What can I do to help?"

"Do you miss me as much
as I miss you?" Still, words
coming out of his mouth
can feel like the first drops
of rain after years lost
in a desperate desert.

It's Jesse's choice for lunch.
Any place that serves
scalding hot chicken fingers
and French fries, apple
juice with ice will do.
Never forget the clipboard,
the task list and marker.
Wait for table, order food,
wait for food, eat food, wait
for everyone to finish, wait
for waitress to bring check,
pay money, wait for change,
walk to car. Click a point,
cross out after each step,
talk about the activity,
take a breath, read schedule
and follow the damn thing
as precisely as possible.

Maybe you're thinking
psychology class, labs
with rats and mazes, Pavlov's
pets. Me too. But sometimes,
what I see is early winter
mornings, a hand rail
to grab as I walk down

icy stairs, my Uncle Dom
with his crutches and braces
that helped him move
from his bed to the living
room, then outside to spend
summer evenings on the front
porch. Now and again,
images of the earth following
its path as it spins around
the sun will fill my mind.

Later, when the worker goes
home and it's just Jesse
and me, we put the clicker
away. He hangs out in his room
tearing thick illustrated dictionaries
into thin strips. I read or write
with music playing softly
in the living room, stop
to look in on him on my way
to the bathroom or kitchen.
He lifts his head, a bit
annoyed, and barely grumbles
something that sounds
like good night. Both of us
at ease, waiting for sleep
and believing that the pieces
of the world will all be
where they belong tomorrow.

WAR STORIES

When we're all sitting
around waiting for yellow
buses to pull up to the curb,
drop the guys off from day
program or watching TV
waiting for ten o'clock
and the night shift to take
our place, sometimes talk
turns to back in the day:
The first time they came over
for lunch, how Jimmy fit
an entire Big Mac in his mouth,
the special sauce spraying
the table like a hydrant
on the summer's hottest day
and Liz shaking her head
whispering he's gonna be
a shit load of trouble. I smiled,
knowing he wasn't assigned
to me. That Sunday afternoon
when Raphael, the worker
you'd least want to see walking
toward you on a late night
empty street, fell asleep
and Jimmy spread his feces
through Raphael's perfectly
picked afro. Jose promising
to take Jimmy to the hookers
on Third Avenue for a half
and half on his twenty-first
birthday. The quiet summer
morning Jean started screaming
and I flew down the stairs,
saw her leaning over Jimmy's

bed trying to wake him,
yelling come on boy, breathe.
She grabbed his shoulders,
and I took his legs. We lifted,
carried him to the floor
and stretched him flat
on his back. I tilted
his chin, cleared his airway,
covered his mouth with mine
and blew, then compressed
his chest while she counted
over and over until
the paramedics clattered
up the stairs. I stood
in the doorway, out
of breath, tasting
his vomit, sweat stinging
my eyes, almost crying
when the medics gave up
on Jimmy, the one guy
I never learned to like.

BLESSINGS

These days we make
appointments to play
slow motion basketball
in Long Island City, sit
on benches to catch
our breath and guzzle
bottled water while we talk
about my calves swelling
like a pregnant woman's,
taking Lasix and pissing every
fifteen minutes until Tom
breaks in, begins to tell us
about last Thursday, walking
down some specialist's long
hallway for the second time,
jerking off to vintage black
and white porn, trying
to find out if it's his sperm
preventing him and his girlfriend
from going forth, multiplying.

Grot describes the screams
and moans his wife made
in the delivery room,
how scared he felt holding
his daughter the first time,
worrying he might drop
the tiny slippery thing
and realizing he knew
nothing about raising
a kid, that he was saying
a final goodbye to his old
simple life as he watched
the doctor stitch the C section

closed. He winces, picks up
the basketball and starts
telling us how he rushes
home every day from work
and he and his wife lie quietly
on their queen sized bed
with their dark haired girl
between them, asleep, forming
some kind of blessed trinity.

We take the court for the last
game of the day thinking
of friends and siblings
who feel desperately helpless
as a son flounders through
first grade already wondering
if he's good enough, a daughter
shutting her bedroom door
struggling not to cut herself.
My friends know all about my ex-
girlfriend and her autistic son
who rarely speaks and only
in quick brash phrases when
he sees something he wants
to touch or eat immediately.
They know I flew into Portland,
spent the July 4th weekend
with him and they both nodded,
understood how much it meant
when driving back to the airport
Jesse leaned forward, tapped
his mom's shoulder, clearly
said, "Tony, come back August."

FAMILY

Sitting around the dinner
table, I imagine you've wondered,
once or twice, every night,
whether you were adopted?
Maybe a bored, over worked nurse
placed you in the wrong crib
the evening you were pried
out of your mother's belly.
Your father could have found you
on an upstate hunting trip
at the mouth of a river nestled
in a basket, or some terrified
fifteen year old girl wrapped
you in a navy blue ski jacket
and left you on the back porch
next to bundles of tied together
newspapers. They took you in,
looked at you as a gift or burden
from god and did their best
to nurture you, torture you
in the name of love and family.

Even during today's Sunday
visit, look to your left, the right,
across the table. If you take
a deep enough breath, the smell
of pot is a fog rising off your sister's
tan wrinkled skin. Your brother
holds forth like Archie Bunker's
mentor on sports and race,
celebrity gossip, his five
fucking cats. And god bless
your baby brother, his wife,
two adorable young kids,

working too many hours
downtown in a corner office
overlooking the construction
of The Freedom Tower in risk
management and rooting
for the Yankees, checking
his cell phone every few minutes
to keep track of fantasy leagues.

But you, you're the weird one,
too quiet, with your writing
and reading, alone, no new
girlfriend, that autistic kid
you still visit in Maine
and now this kidney condition
that you don't like talking about.
Except the medication didn't help
and you will eventually, inevitably
need a transplant and siblings
have the best chance of matching.
Using your distant measured news
caster voice, you recite the facts,
describe the procedure, the risks,
success rate and after care, hope
that one of them will love you
enough or feel obligated enough
to consider it and step forward,
help you maybe live a little longer.

A GOOD BAD DAY

John walks slowly up the stairs
to my office every day. Between
four and four-thirty, after the bus
brings him home from day program
and after he uses the bathroom,
he says, "Oh, hello Tony," as if
he's surprised to find me
sitting at my desk. He says
he had a good day, stands
by a chair and after six years
of living at the residence,
his home, he still hesitates,
wonders if he needs permission
to sit down. I don't give it,
wait until he sits on his own.
He tells me if he read or colored,
exercised or sang today and I ask
questions as if I was his mother.
Maybe he went to a park, a store,
the library. All along he wears
this pleasant, half smiling,
perfectly balanced, zen-like gaze
across his Fred Flintstone face
and I don't know if I'm stressed
or bored, mean, or just a smart-ass
acting like we are friends;
but when he asks me about my day
sometimes I tell him the truth.

Uselessly endless meetings, piles
of paper work, asshole administrators.
Not enough sleep. Girlfriend trouble.
Yesterday, I told him that a woman
I loved is getting married on a boat

in September and I wished
I owned a torpedo. He didn't say
anything, just sat there smiling
and I'm sorry, but I couldn't help it,
I had to ask him if he ever
had a bad day. When he said no,
none that he could remember,
I don't think so and looked like
he was thinking hard. I leaned
forward, said that I felt very sad
when my father died and I wondered
how he felt when his mom and dad
passed away. John jutted out his chin,
looked beyond me and said yeah
that was a bad day. When I asked
if he missed them, he chewed
on his lips, said sometimes,
and I said I know what you mean.

SOCIAL STORY

Now that I am sick
with this kidney condition
I can't spell or pronounce,
my ex girlfriend is worried,
a little about me, but mainly
about her son Jesse.
She wants me to write
a short social story explaining
what death and dying means.
Something somewhat concrete
and not too frightening
that he and his autistic brain
has a chance to grasp.
Something about not being
there any more physically,
but still with him, a part
of him, like blood and bones,
all the time and forever.
Something to prepare him
if and when I need to stop
visiting suddenly. Good luck
I think and begin typing
that some things are hard
to understand and scary
to think about; but learning
about them can sometimes
make things clearer, easier
when they do happen.

One of those things is death
and everybody eventually
dies. Even friends we feel
close to and love, die.
Some people get sick

and never get better
and some people grow
old and die. I write down
no one knows what happens
when people die. But when
we can't hang out and see
our friends anymore, we feel
sad and bad and sometimes
we cry. The good thing
is we can always, any time
we want to, think about them
and how happy and lucky
it made us feel to know
we had someone we loved
who loved us back as much
as anything in the world.
I sign it love, Tony, in big
multicolored block letters,
find an envelope, press on
a super hero stamp, walk
to the corner mailbox.

HARDLY TALKING

Last time I stopped
at the corner Bodega
for coffee, a corn muffin,
the fat woman who always
sits behind the counter
spoke to me in English
for the first time and told me
Emmanuel had died
last week. "You know,"
she said, "The old man."
And I nodded. Larry's friend,
the old guy who straddled
the milk crate, guarded
the outside fruit bins.
Anytime we walked by,
he'd stand and smile, slap
Larry's hand five, take off
his cap. They would hold
each other's shoulders, bow
just a bit and bump heads
gently, three times. Sometimes
he handed Larry a mango
or a zip-locked bag of berries
and I would act like my father,
remind him to say thank you.
When I said I was sorry, that
he seemed like a good man,
she told me to tell Larry.

Larry wears the same grey
sweat shirt every day.
He hides it every night,
fights to keep it out
of the wash, then sneaks

down the basement, listens
to it rinse, tumble dry.
He's thirty seven years old
and can never fall asleep
until that shirt is folded
in his top drawer. I know
that every time we walk
past the store, Larry will
still interlock his forefingers,
keep repeating "my friend,
my friend" with that slurred
slightly raised last syllable
hanging in the air. I'll try
to hurry him, take his hand,
bribe him with a popsicle,
a black and white cookie,
until I'll give up and lie,
promise, that yes, his friend
will be back tomorrow.

The last time I saw
my father, we hardly
talked. I straightened
out his sheets, ate half
of his hospital hamburger
and hoped he would hurry
and fall asleep. I kept
leaning out the door,
checking the clock above
the water fountain, looking
down the hall for my sister
who finally came and took
my place. I left, caught

an early movie and sat
in a nearly empty theater,
watching a movie I can never
remember the name of,
wishing I was Steve Buscemi
making out with his friend's
seventeen year old daughter,
Chloe Sevigny, the night
my father died.

THIS KIND OF ROOM

It's that kind of soft, not too hot, summer day
when all I want to do is be young enough
to run fast break full courts until night falls.
I don't want to subway into the city, stop
in book stores, thumb through bins of used
vinyl for hours, stand in line at the Angelica,
watch one of those movies where I don't care
if the main character lives or dies. I don't
want to be back in love with Erica, driving
to some quaint upstate town, windows
down, in complete control of the tape deck
and we're both singing along as loud
and as off key as we please: Springsteen,
Beach Boys, old live 1969 Poco. Don't want
to linger over brunch, wander into tiny shops
filled with scented candles and antiques,
not even if we stop at a roadside park,
find a deserted shady spot, spread a blanket
and end up making out like when we first met.
I want to be the first and only guy at the schoolyard,
feel the grooves of the ball with my fingertips,
hear it echo off the handball walls, the four
floors of empty brick classrooms, as I take
a few dribbles, make easy lay ups. I don't want
to be in Vermont, back in love with Helen
at the Champlain Valley county fair watching
Jesse stroke some bored cow, taking pictures
as he rides the long rainbow slide fifty-five
straight times no matter how cute and ecstatic
he looks every time. Don't care if he sleeps
through the night and we cuddle through
some video, walk to the bedroom for slow
mind blowing sex and an early morning
rewind. I want to stand at the foul line,

hit a few shots, watch the ball softly fall
through the not yet stolen net. No, not
a little kid on a back in Brooklyn Sunday,
my grandfather, my father, still alive, mom
complaining there's nowhere to place
the lasagna pan and my favorite uncle, Dom,
with his crutches by his side always saying
just as long as there's this kind of room
in heaven, we'll all be alright. I want to nod
knowingly, maybe slap palms, flick bounce
passes when the other guys start showing up,
talking shit, late night west coast box scores.
I definitely don't want to be sitting inside
at my desk, clicking through emails, reading
about my old schoolyard friend Duden's
kidney transplant and how it all went well,
he's recovering nicely. Don't want to think
about my own kidney condition especially
since it's now official that the medication
didn't work. I don't want to spend a moment
making a list of who would contemplate donating
a kidney for me, who would get sick of visiting
me in the hospital first. Today, all I want to do
is shoot for sides. Duden's my first pick. He grabs
a rebound, hits me with an outlet pass. I glide
down the sideline, cross over, take off and soar
to the hoop. Even if my shot somehow rims, spills
out, the Dude will tip it back in, fill the basket.

PILGRIMAGE

Think of the time you flew
into Albuquerque, the drive
from the airport, flat thirsty
red brown land spreading
in all directions, a snow capped
mountain sitting on the horizon,
the adobe village, an old Navajo
driving a creaky bus up hill,
reciting rehearsed facts, wounded
jokes meant for white folks
as the sun blistered down on ancient
dwellings haunted by ghosts
of dry boned medicine men,
young women who fled to the city,
bread frying over a high flame.

The faded purple Acamo t-shirt
is now tucked in your bottom
drawer. You were taking a breath,
running from your most recent
heart wreck, trying to learn
what it would mean to leave
behind a boy, Jesse, you treated
as your only son, some future
you dreamed of building. After
learning how deep a night could grow
without New York City lights,
you woke early and drove hours
to stand in line with shuffling, hunched
over old women who twisted,
entwined strings of black beads
in their fingers as Japanese tourists
dangled cameras from their necks.

You sat in a back pew, watched
the women light candles, kneel,
then fervently trace the sign
of the cross while you remembered
the legend of a bursting hillside
light and a local priest finding
the miraculous crucifix
of Our Lord of Esquipulos
in the famished ground,
carrying it to Santa Cruz,
only to have it disappear
three times and return
unexplainably to the place
it was first discovered.

You ducked into the sacristy,
the sacred sand pit, its walls
lined and cluttered with discarded
braces and crutches, hand
made shrines attesting
to its many miracles.
As women with tears shining
on grateful faces prayed,
you grabbed a fistful of dust,
placed it in a see-through
sandwich baggie, slipped it
into the shirt pocket covering
your heart, and later hid it
in your satchel for the flight home.

Further back, you're the first son
of your family's second generation
born in America. Grandparents, uncles,

119

aunts and cousins celebrated
your every breath as God's
gracious gift until you turned
four years old and your legs
grew into heavy, dead weight
that hurt anytime you walked
anywhere. Your parents, fearing
polio like your Uncle Dom,
went to early morning Masses,
lit green novena candles
and started collecting money
to send you on a pilgrimage
to Lourdes. Doctors took countless
tests, kept you in a hospital
for six months where nuns
somberly patrolled the halls
and the kid in the next bed,
an orphan, with one wooden leg,
one wooden arm, and a pirate hook
for a hand, somehow had the same
last name as yours. Your parents
brought both him and you gifts,
talked of taking him home too
as you grew sick with jealousy.
When they finally gave a label
to your disease, they cured it
with a Frankenstein boot,
a leg brace and hours,
months of physical therapy
that made you stick out,
a cripple, separated from the rest
of the neighborhood kids
and the money was spent

on a station wagon to drive
back and forth to clinic visits.

Then yesterday, after a technician
with a hard to understand
Russian accent kept asking you
to breathe in, breathe out,
hold it, now breathe regularly
while tracing, rubbing
a tiny camera over your chest
and belly in a chilly room
for too long, the cardiologist
proclaimed your aorta was too
wide, susceptible to a rupture
that could instantly kill you
like the actor who starred
in that crappy seventies sitcom
"Three's Company." He described
the procedure, the high rate
of success and the surgeon
as a miracle worker with hands
like God, an enlightened plumber,
replacing a pipe, tightening a valve.

Stunned by the news, you sat
silently. On the subway home,
you remembered the actor's name,
John Ritter, and remembered
how good he was in *Sling Blade*
and you wished that you still
believed in any kind of God
sometimes. You wished
you didn't have to tell your mom

or miss another visit with Jesse,
wished you remembered a plumber
other than Dan Akyroyd bent
beneath an over flowing sink
on a lonely Saturday night,
the crack of his ass peeking
over the top of his pants,
poised for the next straight line,
laughing at you for ever
feeling indestructible, safe.

WORLD OF WONDERS

These days, riding the city bus
is Jesse's favorite activity.
Even if he ends up getting
a Ben and Jerry's brownie
and two slices of Ken's pizza
where he eats the cheese
while I munch on his crust,
it's the journey that matters.
He always sits on the same spot
of the bench, patiently waits.
Whether it's wintry and windy,
sunny and steamy, he never moves
to the shade or the glass shelter.
He loves watching cars glide by,
sliding his special pass in the slot
to pay, sitting by a window, feeling
the drum and hum beneath his feet.
Giddy sounds bubble, tumble out
of his mouth and everyone looks
at him, then quickly turns away
whenever I catch them staring.

In small cities, buses are filled
mostly with people too poor
to afford cars, old ladies muttering
nonsense through clenched teeth,
unemployed hung over guys
and broken women heading
to shelters with a toddler
or two, and Jesse and me. Today
the fattest woman I've ever seen
hauls herself onto the bus carrying
a tiny child, a folded carriage.
She plops down taking up two

and a half seats. Nearby riders
scatter to the back as if a mortar
shell just landed. She thanks them
in a voice just beyond a whisper.
I'm sorry and I know it's cruel,
but I do catch myself trying
to imagine the guy who plunged
himself into that mass of flesh?

The other riders are still sneaking
glances at Jesse and I wonder
what they would think if they knew
the whole story. They'd understand
how I once loved his mom and took
Jesse, five years old at the time,
as my own. But even close friends
can't believe I travel so far to visit,
wonder if he's my biological son,
did I get any mercy sex this time.
No, I haven't seen Helen in nearly two
years. We set up, coordinate dates
and times in emails as taut and terse
as Raymond Carver characters
and I don't know why she never
wants to spend one second with me
or thank me for anything anymore.
Jesse's workers' take me to/from
the airport and in between it's him
and me for three days, and I always
give thanks for my time with him.

Back on the bus, the woman's son
bounces on her knee. Too young
to talk, his head bops and shakes

like a bobble head. His brightly lit
eyes, excited and curious, settle
on Jesse and his mouth grows
into a giggle, shows the start of two
tiny front teeth. His mom snuggles
him closer and lightly kisses the top
of his head and her skin shines
like a halo. Later, when Jesse lifts
my bags out of the trunk, starts
to walk back to the car, I ask for a hug
and he leans in, lends me his cheek
as usual. When I say, a real hug,
he extends his arms straight out
like the wings of an airplane, a huge
bird anxious for flight. But before
he turns to walk away, I say no,
this time I want a squeeze. He wraps
his arms around me and I am filled
with wonder for the ten whole
seconds he can stand to hold me.

KNOWLEDGE

Larry's not smart enough
to know he's retarded.
He's unaware he's built
like a bowling pin,
that his shaved head shines
like Mr. Clean and everybody
stares when he waddles
down the block. He's happy
holding my hand, crossing
the street to eat pizza.
We order a large pie, slide
in a booth and wait for Nancy.
Larry blows a wolf whistle
when we kiss and I fit
my tongue into her mouth.
He eats three slices, slurps
the cheese stringing down
his chin, sucks the sauce
off his fingers and sips
Pepsi. Every loud burp
is a gunshot of joy.

Last month, we spent
our first night together.
We stopped at the Bodega,
picked up pieces of fruit,
orange juice and a bunch
of blue flowers. She played
Rickie Lee Jones and we kissed
on the couch like junior high,
tugged at each other's clothes,
moved to the bedroom, lit
candles. We fucked and fucked
until she made me promise

to let her sleep. She wrapped
my arms around her,
curled into me. I stayed
awake, kept watch all night.

I hug Larry goodbye
on the stoop, watch him
walk inside the residence
with his counselor. I know
she'll help him bathe, brush
his teeth, button his pajamas.
She'll tuck him in, shut
the door behind her. Larry
will wait for quiet, pull
down his bottoms and turn
on his stomach. He'll slide
the pillow between his thighs,
bunch it into a ball,
hump it until he comes.
He'll finger paint the silky
thick liquid across his chest,
lift it to his nose, sniff,
then taste it. I don't know
who or what fills his head
these moments. Long lean
blondes? Muscular black
men in motorcycle boots?
Down's Syndrome women
and their light blue eyes,
full floppy breasts? Is his mind
empty like a Buddhist's,
content with the feel of his own
skin, the heat and the speed
building until he reinvents fire?

Larry will probably die
in that Catholic group home
for six men in Brooklyn.
He will never lie down
with a woman, never sleep
next to someone he loves
for seven years, roll together
in the middle of the night,
half asleep, and wake to find
himself moving inside her.
He'll never have to forget
that Sunday morning, the bagels
and hot chocolate, the way
she says she has to talk to him
and she doesn't know where
to begin. She's not sure how
it happened, and she never wanted
to hurt him; but she doesn't
love him anymore and she thinks
she needs to leave. Larry
will never find out how long
it takes to learn to sleep
alone again. And years later
he will never meet someone
new. He will never go
home with her that first
night, never lie awake,
watch her eyelids jerk
as part of some dream
and wonder if tonight
could be the beginning
of something holy.

TO BELIEVE OR NOT TO BELIEVE

On any winter Sunday
I can kneel in a polished
pew, watch a priest raise
a thin wafer, a gold plated
chalice over his head,
believe bread and wine
becomes flesh and blood,
then sit in front of a TV
with my dips and beer
believing the worst team
can beat the best one.

Days later, I can meet
my brother on the steps
of a hospital in Queens, walk
down empty halls, take
the elevator to the basement,
watch a film about drinking,
driving, recovery and putting
faith in a higher power, catch
my brother's eye, shake
my head slightly and try
not to laugh while everyone
praises Jesus and God's plan
as John faces jail time.

I want to believe John
when he says he's sorry,
he's worried about our mom,
what our dead father
would have thought.
I'm afraid he's only sorry
he got caught, worried
how he'll get place to place

without a car, not scared
enough to stop drinking, too
old and lonely to change.

At work, I'm in the middle
of an investigation, trying
to find out if two workers
spent last Saturday night
from 8-9:00, after showers
and medication, having sex
in the bedroom where three
of the retarded guys sleep.
Everyone was talking and
I didn't know who or what
to believe, how to tell
the truth from the lies,
didn't try to imagine
all that's been left out.

Even when me and Suzanne
were completely in love, alone
in the residence, we never
went that far. Maybe a brush
against each other, her hips,
my shoulder, a finger tracing
lips, my hands sliding down
her side, one simple chaste
kiss. Back then I was certain
there was plenty of time,
I believed she'd leave Bill
and we'd end up together.
Now I know how easy
it would have been, how
no one would have known

and I wouldn't spend another
moment trying to imagine
how amazing it would have felt.

Tonight, I want to believe
this beautiful young woman
with the prettiest, darkest eyes
I can ever remember seeing
is looking at me the same way
I am looking at her. Walking
to her favorite nearby restaurant,
sitting at a corner table,
talking about poetry, Bob
and Jakob Dylan, the tattoo
on her wrist. She listens closely,
leans in to tell a secret or two,
describes the chocolate cake
she wants so badly. The waitress
apologizes, explains they never
have any on Mondays. I'm hoping
we'll sit here again, maybe
next Friday night. She'll reach
across, feed me a forkful
and I'll believe it's the best
cake I've ever tasted. This time,
when we linger at the mouth
of the subway, it will turn into
slow kisses, a bumpy uptown
cab ride, a three day weekend.

Of course, I remember opening
that hand written letter
from Helen after eight years

of silence, fitting my own
note in an envelope, walking
to the mail box. I flew
to Maine, talked all night
and day, in and out of bed,
and decided to believe her
when she explained everything
was different and she swore
she'd never hurt me again.
Besides, I was free falling
myself, hurtling toward her
and her son, this beautiful,
fascinating, autistic 5 year old.
Even when it ended harsher
and sadder than the first time,
I wanted to believe that me
and Jesse had connected,
that we meant something
important to each other.

I do my best to stay part
of Jesse's life: sending gifts,
visiting four, five weekends
a year, blowing up air mattresses,
ceaselessly climbing in and out
of their blue car, blindly driving
the endless two lane highways
and back roads that make up
the secret maze mapped out
in the deepest parts of Jesse's
ever anxious heart and mind.
Sometimes, we stop to roll
or sled down hills, swing

in hammocks, eat chicken
fingers, bad Maine pizza,
shoot hoops or ride bikes,
spend days at Great Escape
as Jesse rides every scary ride
in the place twice, never sure
if he ever thinks about me
when I'm back in Brooklyn.

On my last visit, Jesse
sat still, stared at a keyboard
for thirty minutes and typed
out words while a teacher held
his forearm for support, helped
lift his finger after he pecked
each letter. She kept her eye
on the screen too, tightened
or lessened the pressure
on Jesse's arm anytime
he resisted or tried to race
too fast and I wondered
how he could spell words
he needs help to read.

Fifteen, twenty years ago,
Facilitative Communication
was hailed as a miracle
until every objective study
proved it was the helper
guiding the kid's hand
subconsciously. But Helen,
Jesse's teachers and respite
workers are excited about

his progress and I'm hoping
what I believe is wrong.

When Jesse typed
he wanted to talk to me,
I leaned forward. He wrote
he was excited to see me
and I told him I missed him,
asked what he wanted to do
this weekend. He typed
he's glad I keep coming
so far to see him, sometimes
his autism gets in the way
and he can't always show
how he feels, but he types
he thinks I am his dad.

I didn't know what to say.
I wanted to believe
this was Jesse looking
into my eyes, speaking
his own true words.
I took an index card,
printed big capital letters
"I wish I was your father
and you know I'll do
everything I can for you."
I underlined it slowly
with my finger, made
Jesse read it out loud
and hoped he believed me.

MAGNITUDE

My friend's wife has a niece
who's autistic. He doesn't seem
to believe that I never wish
Jesse was different. He talks
about missing the big things
like proms and graduations.
I joke about the perks, not
worrying about Jesse using
nonprescription drugs, driving
drunk on weekends, paying
for college, pretending to like
the woman he wants to marry.
I tell him I take Jesse as he is
and I know what not to expect,
how every new tiny thing
grows in magnitude: the first
time he ran to me, grabbed
my hand when I picked him up
at school, the first morning
he walked into our Brooklyn
bedroom to cuddle between us,
that one time he scavenged
through his cluttered sensations,
strung four words together
and told me clearly, 'Tony
come back August.' I explain
I am one of the chosen few
that Jesse invites into his world
and it helps me imagine
I am special with unique super
powers. But yes, I am lying
a bit. I've always wanted to lift
him on my shoulders, six years
old and singing that he believes

in the promised land at a Springsteen
show, play some one-on-one
in a schoolyard, keeping it
close and never letting him win
until he beats me on his own.
And yes, this past weekend
in Maine, I wished he watched
television. We would have sat
and argued when Girardi
benched A-Rod, ate salty snacks
as the Yanks played the Orioles
in the deciding fifth game.
Instead, I sat on a kitchen stool,
listening to the radio broadcast
while Jesse was happy in his room,
alone, tearing pages of picture books
into piles of thin paper strips.

About the Author

Tony Gloeggler was born in Brooklyn and lives in Queens. He's managed a group home for developmentally disabled men in Boerum Hill for over 35 years. His poems have appeared in numerous journals and anthologies. His chapbook *One on One* received the 1998 Pearl Poetry Prize. Pavement Saw Press published his first full length collection, *One Wish Left,* in 2002. *My Other Life* was published by Jane Street Press in 2004 and *Greatest Hits: 1984-2009* was put out by Pudding House in 2009. *The Last Lie* was published in 2010 by NYQ Books, and Bittersweet Editions has recently published a collaboration between Tony and photographer, Marco North, titled *Tony Come Back August.*

CPSIA information can be obtained
at www.ICGtesting.com
Printed in the USA
FFOW02n0102061015
17465FF

9 781630 450076